# STITCH ⊘ PEOPLE

# BACKGROUNDS

*Scenic patterns and coordinating accessories
to adorn your Stitch People portraits*

## BY ELIZABETH DABCZYNSKI-BEAN, JESSICA SAVAGE & ZANNY DELSAS

© 2019 BEANSKI, LLC
PUBLISHED BY BEANSKI, LLC
WWW.STITCHPEOPLE.COM

ISBN: 978-0-9988236-4-5
©2019 Beanski, LLC

**Author Information:** Elizabeth Dabczynski-Bean is the Founder of Stitch People
Lizzy was raised in upstate New York, has been a "Utah-n" for years, and is now a resident of sunny Southern California. A multipotentialite, or jack-of-all trades, Lizzy majored in Music Business and is currently pursuing "The Dream" of being a full-time actor. She has held jobs in technology education, interior design, theater administration, graphic design, and photography, in addition to owning and running Stitch People. Lizzy enjoys learning about fitness and nutrition, doing home improvement and RV projects, performing musical theater, and volunteering at animal shelters when she can. _Follow Lizzy on Instagram: @lizzydbean_

**Contributing Designer:** Jessica Savage is a regular designer for Stitch People
Jess lives in South Australia, amongst the dangers of Australian wildlife and the blazing summer sun. A recovered musician and recovering research scientist, Jess has returned to her artistic roots in this next chapter of life that sees her don a fancy designer's hat. When not creating patterns, Jess enjoys being clumsy in the outdoors, writing fiction, watching Star Trek on repeat, and singing in the car. Loudly. _Follow Jess on Instagram: @cabsav_

**Contributing Designer:** Zanny Delsas is a contracted designer for Stitch People
Zanny grew up in the PNW of Washington state. As a girl, she learned to cross stitch from her mom - an avid seamstress, quilter, and crafter. Zanny loves to try new crafts, and to decorate her home, mixing styles, colors and patterns. She is also a collector. Beach glass, enamel pins, and Starbucks mugs to name a few. She loves to travel, thrift shopping, and all things related to the beach. Zanny has lived in the mountains of Colorado and on the beach in Costa Rica. She currently resides in the desert of Arizona with her husband James and their rescue pup Will. _Follow Zanny on Instagram: @lefthandedstitcher_

**This book is dedicated to the amazing Stitch People Community, the wonderful ideas that are shared, and the unfettered, genuine expressions of love and encouragement found there.**

Published by Beanski, LLC
info@stitchpeople.com  |  www.StitchPeople.com  |  @stitchpeople

# TABLE OF CONTENTS

# CAMPING & THE WOODS

The pattern below was modeled after the image to the left. The scenery and background utilizes patterns found in this book, in the "Camping & The Woods" section and "Open Sky" section.

The man and woman were created using mix-and-match patterns found in "Do-It-Yourself Stitch People."

Don't forget to get creative with your patterns by adding texture and dimension to things through combining threads and deliberately changing the direction of your stitches. For example, try creating a more natural look with your pine trees by creating a "pine needle" effect that works outward from the center of the tree design. For all stitches to the right of the tree's center, make the top diagonals of your cross-stitches this direction: \\\ - then, for the stitches to the left of center, make all the top diagonals of your cross-stitches this direction: ///. This will create an effect of the "pine needles" following the shape of the tree: ///\\\.

TRUE TO SCALE OF SIZE 11 AIDA FABRIC: 11 SQUARES PER INCH

NOT EVERY PATTERN NEEDS TO BE USED IN IT'S ENTIRETY. TRY "SLICING" THE TREE IN HALF, VERTICALLY, AND POSITIONING IT AT THE FAR RIGHT OR FAR LEFT OF YOUR PORTRAIT, FLUSH WITH THE FRAME.

SOME MOMENTS NEED AN EXTRA SPECIAL MEMENTO.

TRY USING DIFFERENT ELEMENTS FROM THIS BOOK FASHIONED
IN BORDER DESIGNS TO MAKE AN EXTRA SPECIAL PORTRAIT FOR
THOSE EXTRA SPECIAL ACHIEVEMENTS!

Pacific Crest Trail
2018

GO OUTSIDE THE
LINES OF THE AIDA
FABRIC IF NEEDED
TO ACHIEVE THE
LOOK OF PINE
BRANCHES!

On The
Road
Again!

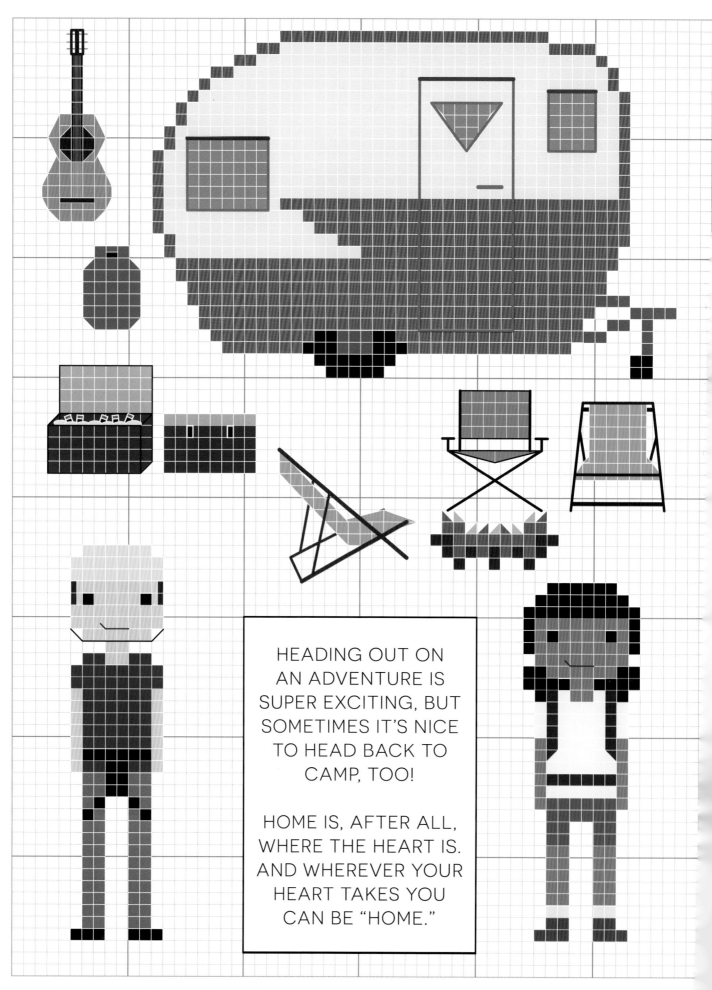

HEADING OUT ON AN ADVENTURE IS SUPER EXCITING, BUT SOMETIMES IT'S NICE TO HEAD BACK TO CAMP, TOO!

HOME IS, AFTER ALL, WHERE THE HEART IS. AND WHEREVER YOUR HEART TAKES YOU CAN BE "HOME."

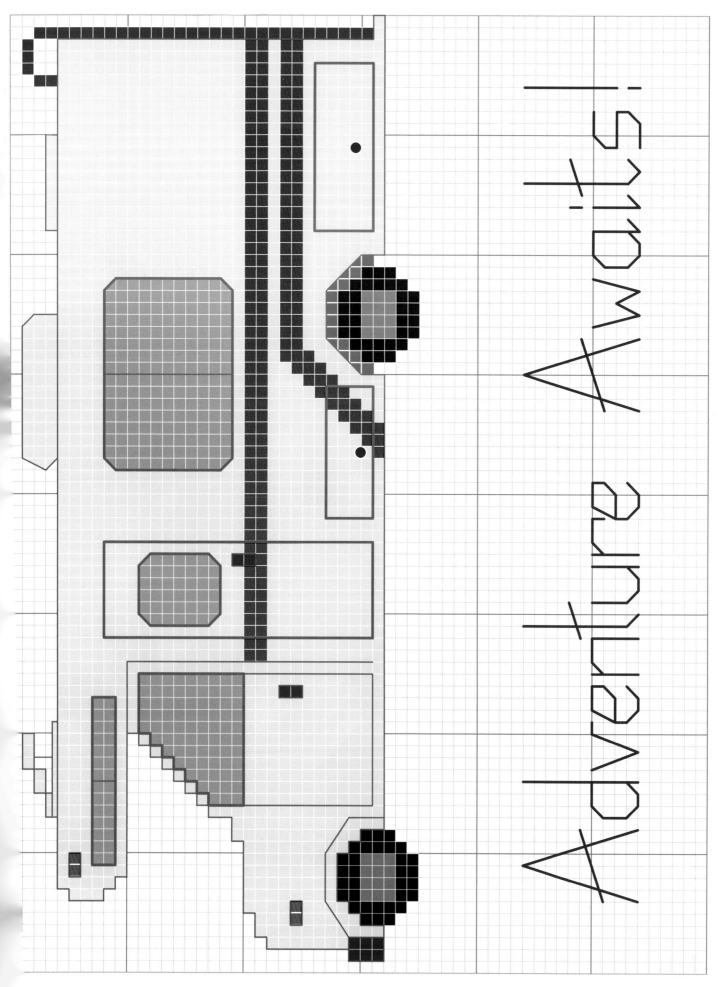

Adventure Awaits!

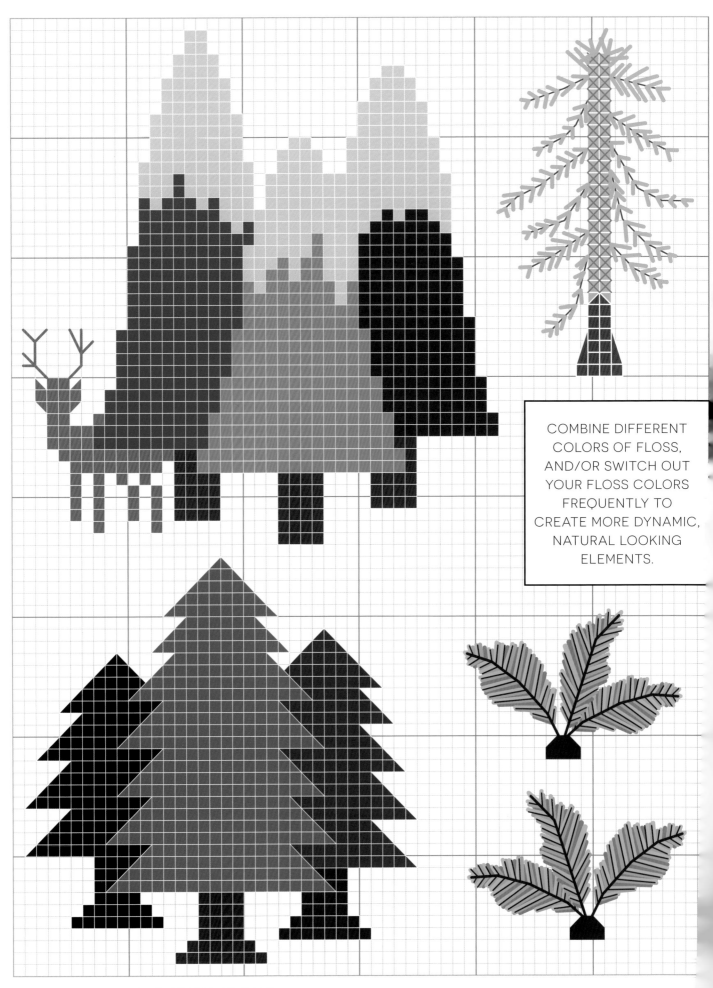

COMBINE DIFFERENT
COLORS OF FLOSS,
AND/OR SWITCH OUT
YOUR FLOSS COLORS
FREQUENTLY TO
CREATE MORE DYNAMIC,
NATURAL LOOKING
ELEMENTS.

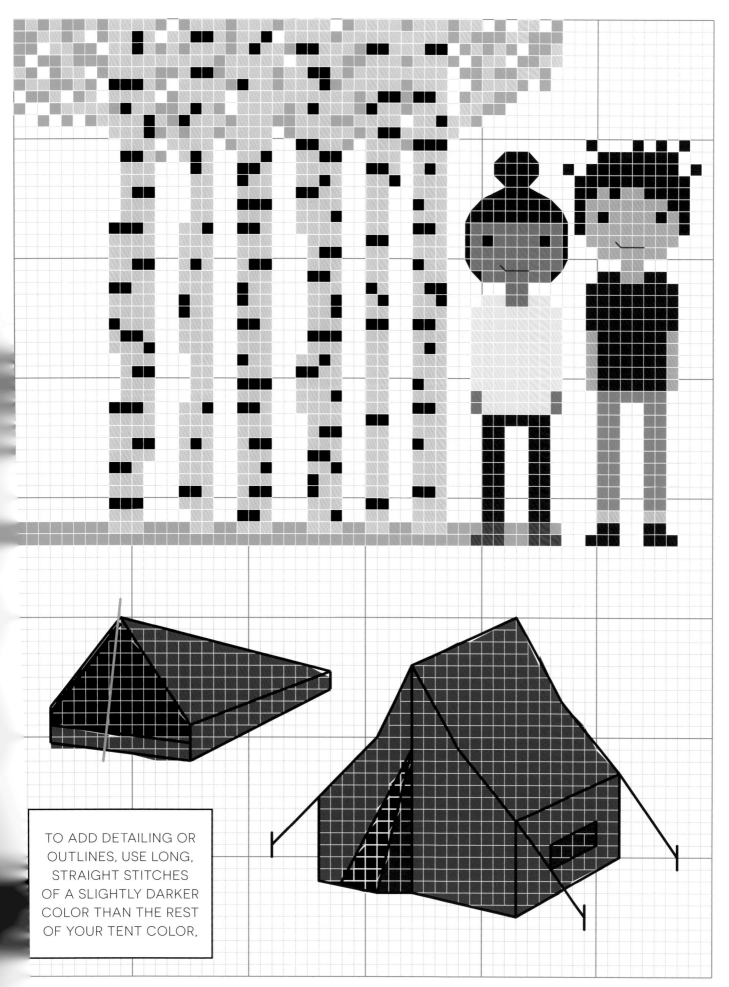

TO ADD DETAILING OR OUTLINES, USE LONG, STRAIGHT STITCHES OF A SLIGHTLY DARKER COLOR THAN THE REST OF YOUR TENT COLOR.

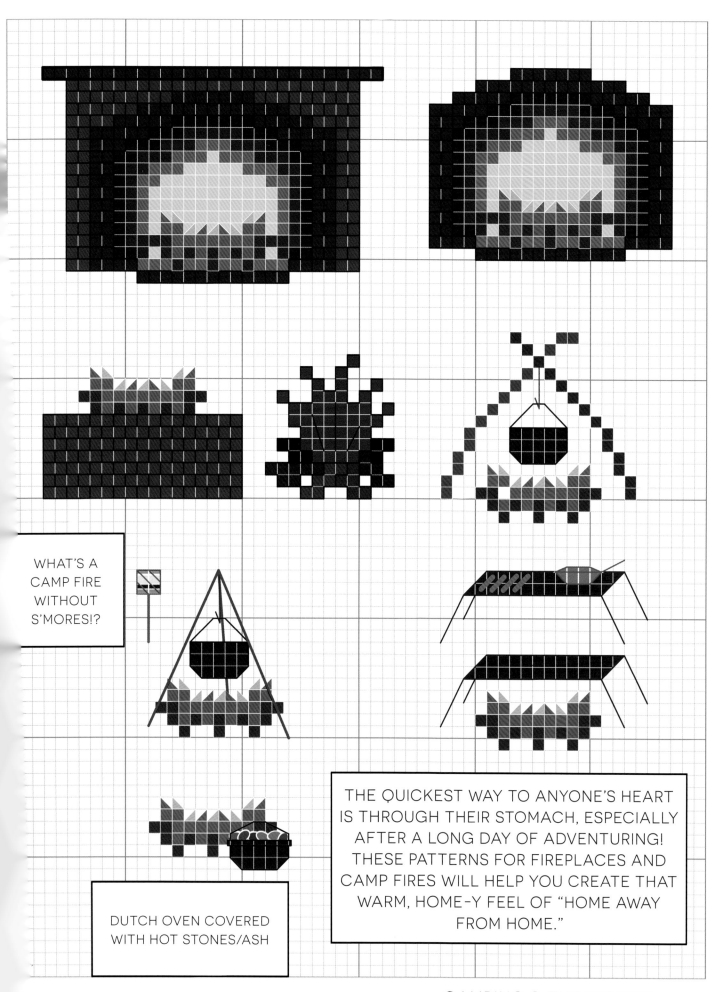

WHAT'S A CAMP FIRE WITHOUT S'MORES!?

DUTCH OVEN COVERED WITH HOT STONES/ASH

THE QUICKEST WAY TO ANYONE'S HEART IS THROUGH THEIR STOMACH, ESPECIALLY AFTER A LONG DAY OF ADVENTURING! THESE PATTERNS FOR FIREPLACES AND CAMP FIRES WILL HELP YOU CREATE THAT WARM, HOME-Y FEEL OF "HOME AWAY FROM HOME."

# USA NATIONAL PARKS

The pattern below was modeled after the image to the left. The scenery and background utilizes patterns found in this book, in the "USA National Parks" section, the "Open Sky" section, and the "Camping & The Woods" section (the bushes utilize the large, autumn tree pattern but with light, medium, and dark hues of green instead of yellow, orange and red). The couple was created by mixing and matching patterns from "Do-It-Yourself Stitch People."

When creating your backgrounds, remember you do not have to copy every element of a scene exactly. Relax! The point is to allude to the element closely enough to paint a picture, so to speak, and jog the memory of the viewer who will enjoy the Stitch People portrait for years and years to come.

TRUE TO SCALE OF SIZE 11 AIDA FABRIC: 11 SQUARES PER INCH

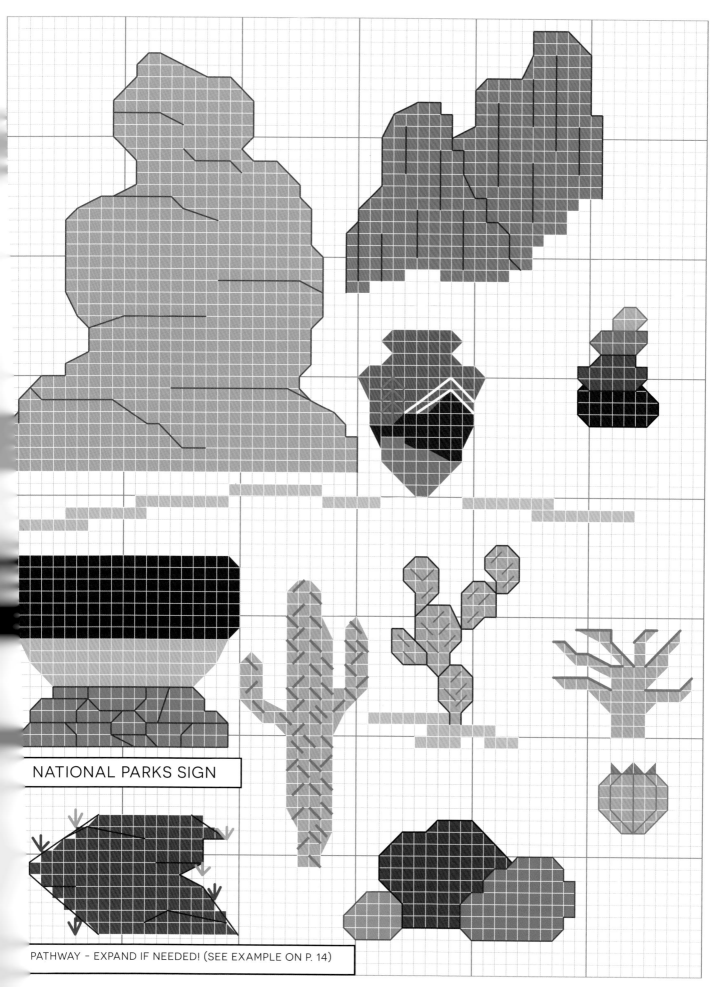

NATIONAL PARKS SIGN

PATHWAY - EXPAND IF NEEDED! (SEE EXAMPLE ON P. 14)

ARCHES NATIONAL PARK, UTAH

TRY LAYERING YOUR CHARACTERS IN FRONT OF THE SMALLER BACKGROUND ELEMENTS TO CREATE A SENSE OF DISTANCE.

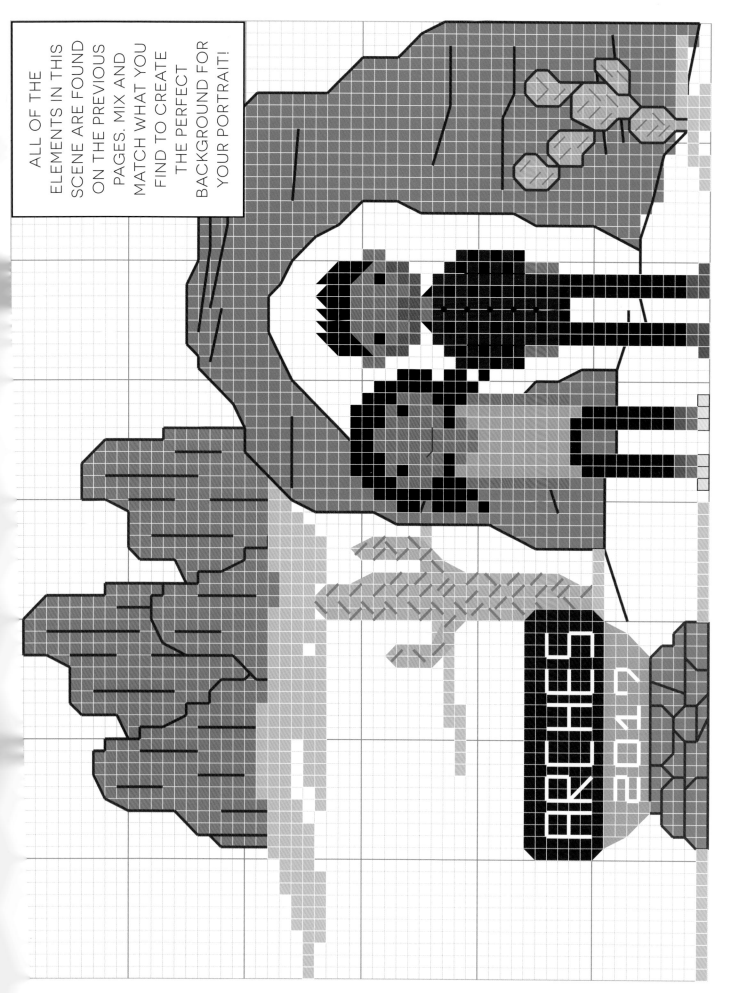

ALL OF THE ELEMENTS IN THIS SCENE ARE FOUND ON THE PREVIOUS PAGES. MIX AND MATCH WHAT YOU FIND TO CREATE THE PERFECT BACKGROUND FOR YOUR PORTRAIT!

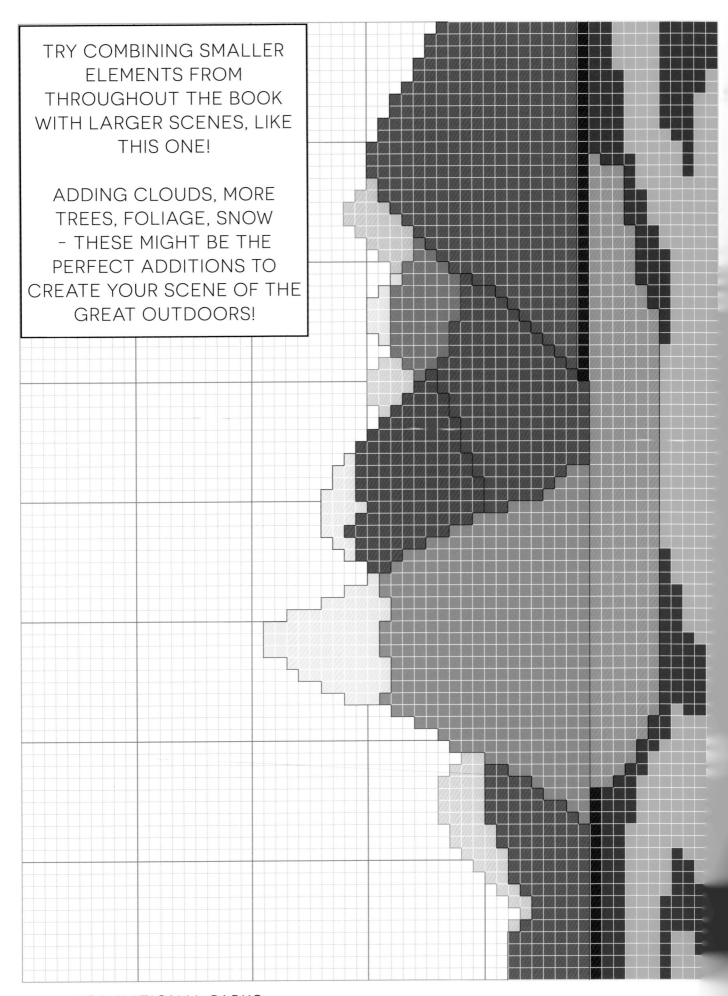

TRY COMBINING SMALLER ELEMENTS FROM THROUGHOUT THE BOOK WITH LARGER SCENES, LIKE THIS ONE!

ADDING CLOUDS, MORE TREES, FOLIAGE, SNOW - THESE MIGHT BE THE PERFECT ADDITIONS TO CREATE YOUR SCENE OF THE GREAT OUTDOORS!

SOMETIMES IT'S HARD TO ARTICULATE JUST HOW MUCH YOU LOVE SOMEONE.
REDWOOD TREES CAN LIVE MORE THAN A THOUSAND YEARS: HOW ABOUT
STITCHING YOUR INITIALS OR A SMALL HEART INTO A CROSS-STITCHED REDWOOD?
(BUT DON'T CARVE INTO A **REAL** REDWOOD - PRESERVE OUR WILD LAND!)

THE PINE TREES IN THIS PORTRAIT WOULD BE CREATED WITH STRAIGHT, DIAGONAL STITCHES GOING OUTWARD FROM THE CENTER OF THE PINE TREE.

BASS HARBOR HEAD LIGHTHOUSE, ACADIA NATIONAL PARK, MAINE

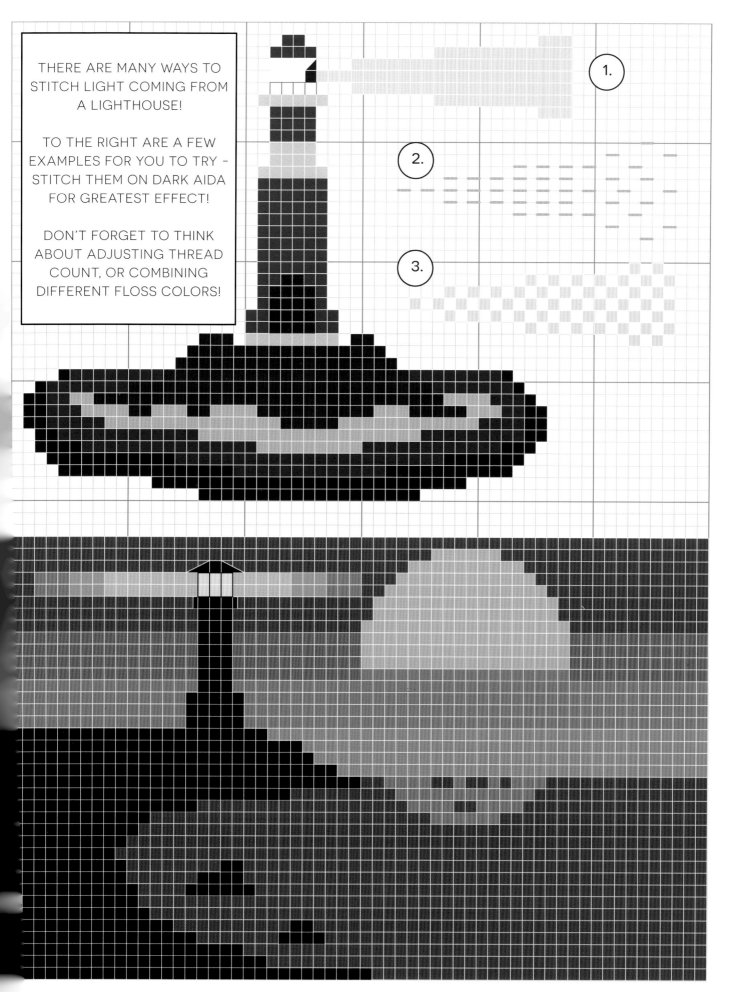

THERE ARE MANY WAYS TO STITCH LIGHT COMING FROM A LIGHTHOUSE!

TO THE RIGHT ARE A FEW EXAMPLES FOR YOU TO TRY - STITCH THEM ON DARK AIDA FOR GREATEST EFFECT!

DON'T FORGET TO THINK ABOUT ADJUSTING THREAD COUNT, OR COMBINING DIFFERENT FLOSS COLORS!

1.

2.

3.

# GEYSERS

TO CREATE THE LOOK OF WATER, MIX AND/OR COMBINE FLOSS COLORS OF GRAY, BLUE, OFF-WHITE, AND WHITE.

FOR AN EXTRA "POP," STITCH YOUR PORTRAIT ON OFF-WHITE OR DARK AIDA FABRIC.

CREATE DETAIL WITH A SINGLE THREAD OF LIGHTLY COLORED FLOSS.

# OPEN SKY

The pattern below was modeled after the image to the left. The scenery utilizes patterns found in this book, in the "Open Sky" section, the "Beachy & Tropical" section, and the "Snowy Scenes" section (the snowboard was used to create the wake-board.) The wet-suit pattern can be found in "Do-It-Yourself-Stitch People," and the kite was created from scratch, by following the shape of the kite as shown in the image to the left.

Your scenes and backgrounds can be as complicated or as simple as you'd like. In this pattern, simple lines, shapes and colors create a scene that is instantly recognizable as the photograph shown here.

Do not be overwhelmed by the amount of detail you believe you must include - it's entirely up to you, and simple choices can be very effective! Better to have a finished, simpler piece than a complicated piece that takes five years to complete!

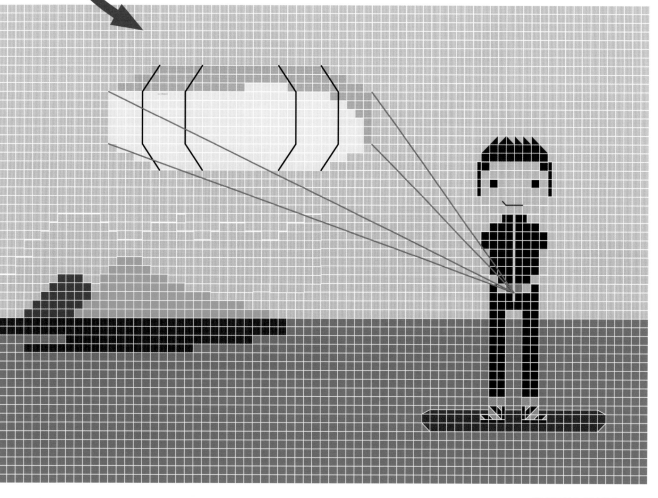

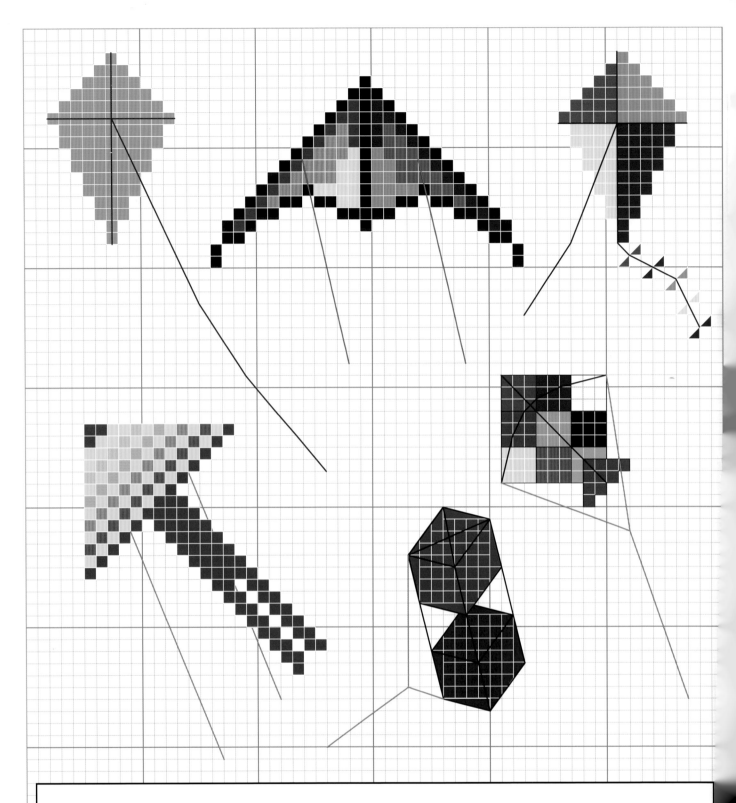

THERE'S SOMETHING UTTERLY MAGICAL ABOUT KITES IN A CLEAR BLUE SKY! THE COLORS, THE MOVEMENT, THE WHIMSY – I'VE NEVER SEEN A SAD FACE AT A KITE FESTIVAL!

IF YOU'RE A FAN OF THESE FLYING MACHINES, TRY USING THESE PATTERNS TO FILL YOUR PORTRAIT SKIES!

SOME MOMENTS MAKE IMPACTS THAT LAST A LIFETIME.

WHATEVER IT IS THAT IMPACTS YOU - THE THING THAT FUELS YOUR FIRE - SHARE IT WITH THOSE YOU LOVE. PERHAPS THEY'LL FEEL THAT SAME PASSION BURN FOR THE VERY SAME MEMORY.

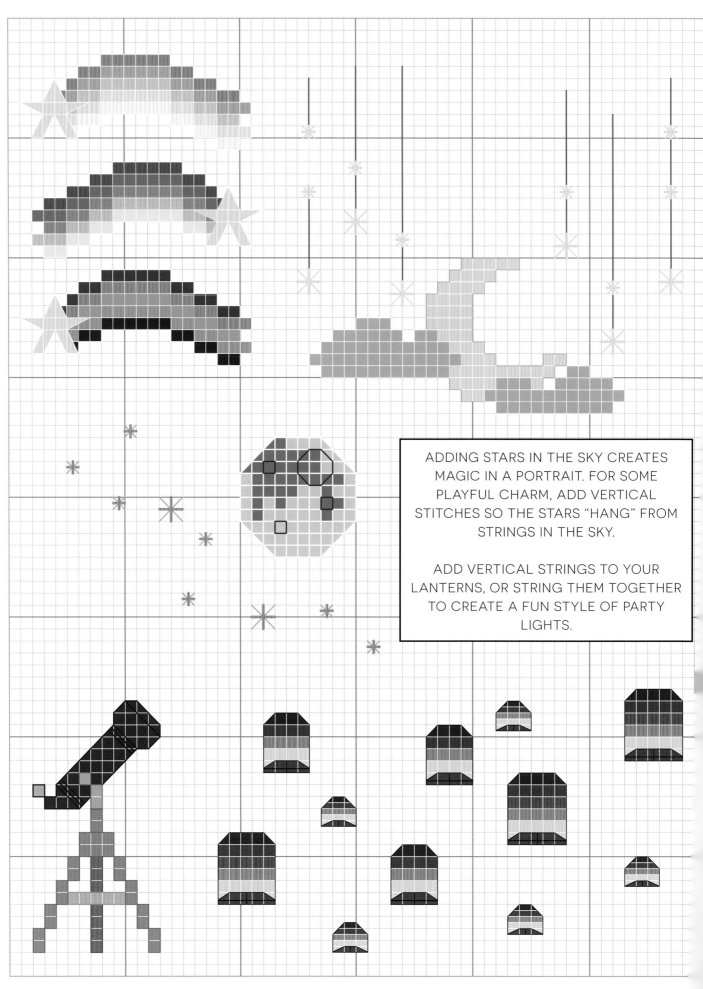

ADDING STARS IN THE SKY CREATES MAGIC IN A PORTRAIT. FOR SOME PLAYFUL CHARM, ADD VERTICAL STITCHES SO THE STARS "HANG" FROM STRINGS IN THE SKY.

ADD VERTICAL STRINGS TO YOUR LANTERNS, OR STRING THEM TOGETHER TO CREATE A FUN STYLE OF PARTY LIGHTS.

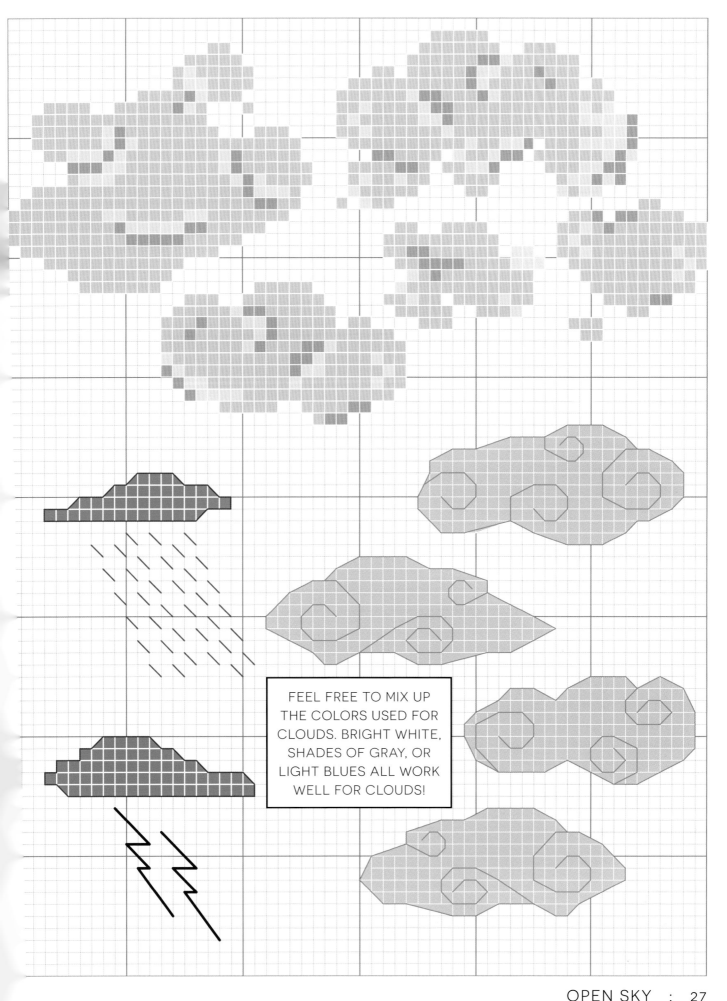

FEEL FREE TO MIX UP
THE COLORS USED FOR
CLOUDS. BRIGHT WHITE,
SHADES OF GRAY, OR
LIGHT BLUES ALL WORK
WELL FOR CLOUDS!

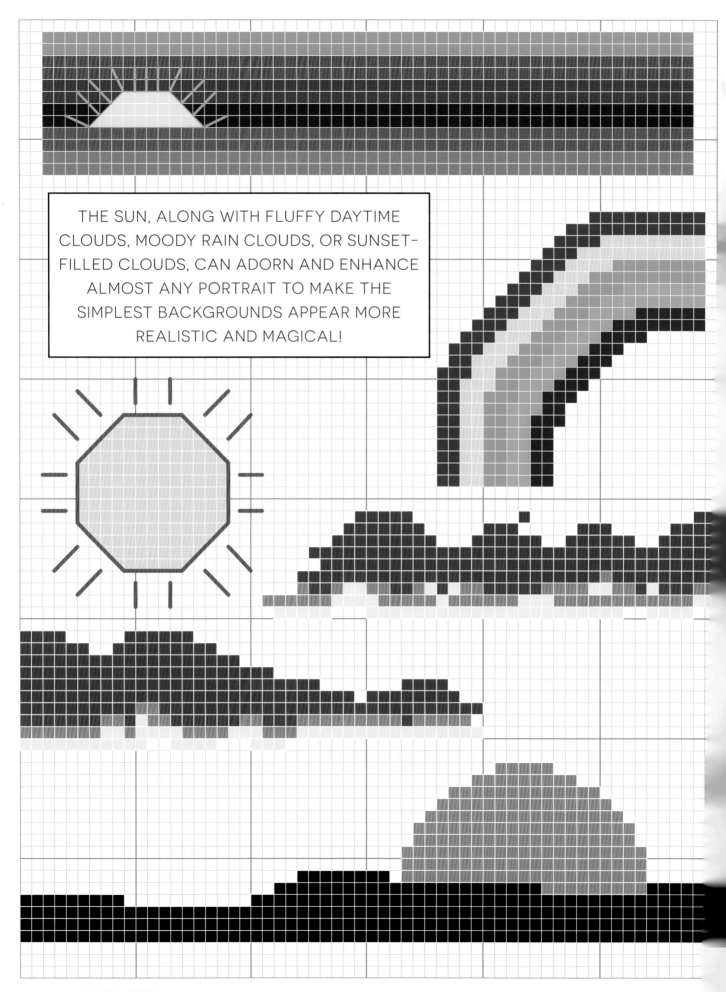

THE SUN, ALONG WITH FLUFFY DAYTIME CLOUDS, MOODY RAIN CLOUDS, OR SUNSET-FILLED CLOUDS, CAN ADORN AND ENHANCE ALMOST ANY PORTRAIT TO MAKE THE SIMPLEST BACKGROUNDS APPEAR MORE REALISTIC AND MAGICAL!

# GARDENS & OUTDOOR PARTIES

The pattern below was modeled after the image to the left. The scenery utilizes patterns found in this book, in the "Open Sky" section, the "Beachy & Tropical" section, and the "Gardens & Outdoor Parties" section. The characters were created using patterns from "Do-It-Yourself-Stitch People." Circles were added to allude to the need for more French knots than some of the patterns in the "Gardens & Outdoor Parties" section include.

Do not let French knots scare you! Practice makes perfect, and putting in a little extra time to learn how to complete these stitches can make a huge difference in the amount of detail you can include in your Stitch People portraits. Large, loose French knots combined with smaller, tighter French knots can create lovely interest and contrast to your portraits. Check out our French knot tutorial! https://stitchpeople.com/frenchknot

PUT THOSE FRENCH KNOTS TO GOOD USE TO CREATE FLOWERS AND VEGETABLES!

TO MAKE YOUR GREENHOUSE LOOK AS THOUGH IT HAS GLASS PANELS, TRY REPLACING A PLANT'S BRIGHT COLORS WITH SLIGHTLY MUTED/GRAYISH VERSIONS OF THAT COLOR WHEN PLANTS ARE TO APPEAR AS THOUGH THEY'RE BEHIND GLASS.

HAND SHOVEL STUCK IN THE GROUND

TO CREATE LAVENDER FRONDS, USE A SINGLE STRAND OF FLOSS FOR BOTH THE FLOWERS AND THE STEMS, CREATING SIMPLE, SLIGHTLY DIAGONAL STITCHES GOING OUTWARD FROM THE VASE.

IF YOU HAVE A KNACK FOR INTRICATE STITCHING, YOU CAN TRY ADDING THE INDIVIDUAL LEAVES AND FLOWERS.

YOU CAN TRY USING A FEW SMALL FRENCH KNOTS IN A VERTICAL LINE FOR THE FLOWERS, AND STRAIGHT STITCHES FOR THE STEMS.

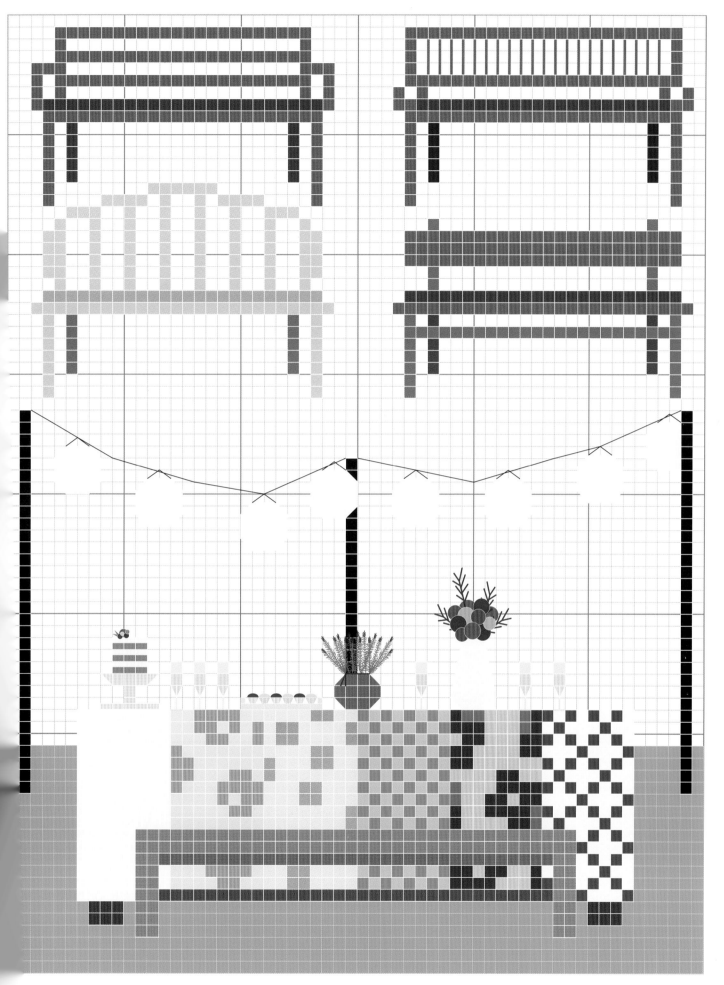

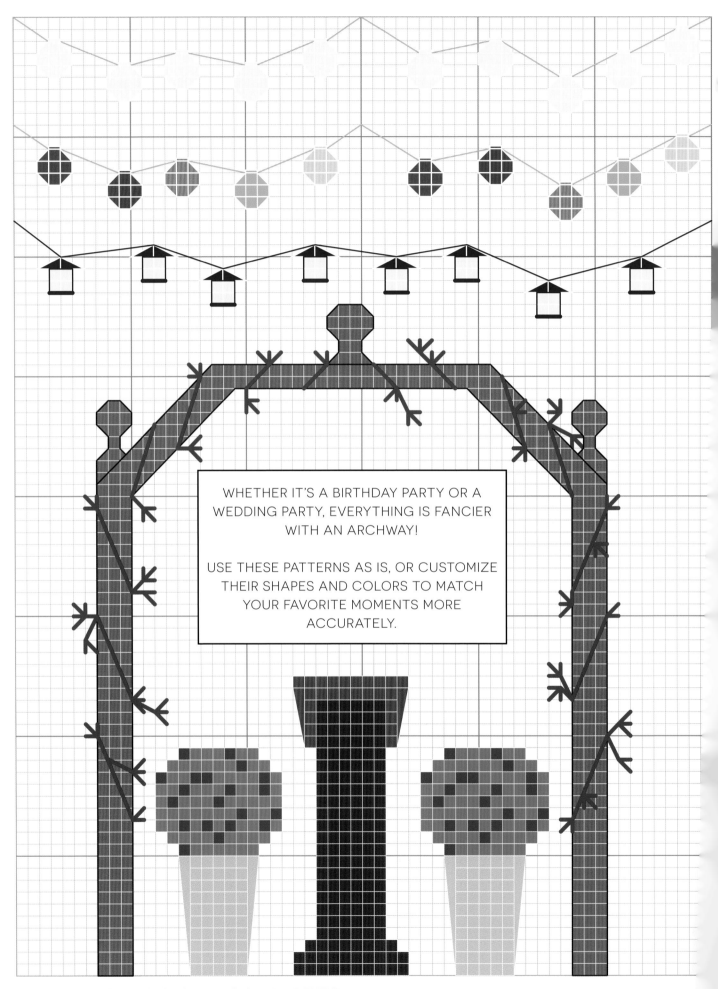

WHETHER IT'S A BIRTHDAY PARTY OR A WEDDING PARTY, EVERYTHING IS FANCIER WITH AN ARCHWAY!

USE THESE PATTERNS AS IS, OR CUSTOMIZE THEIR SHAPES AND COLORS TO MATCH YOUR FAVORITE MOMENTS MORE ACCURATELY.

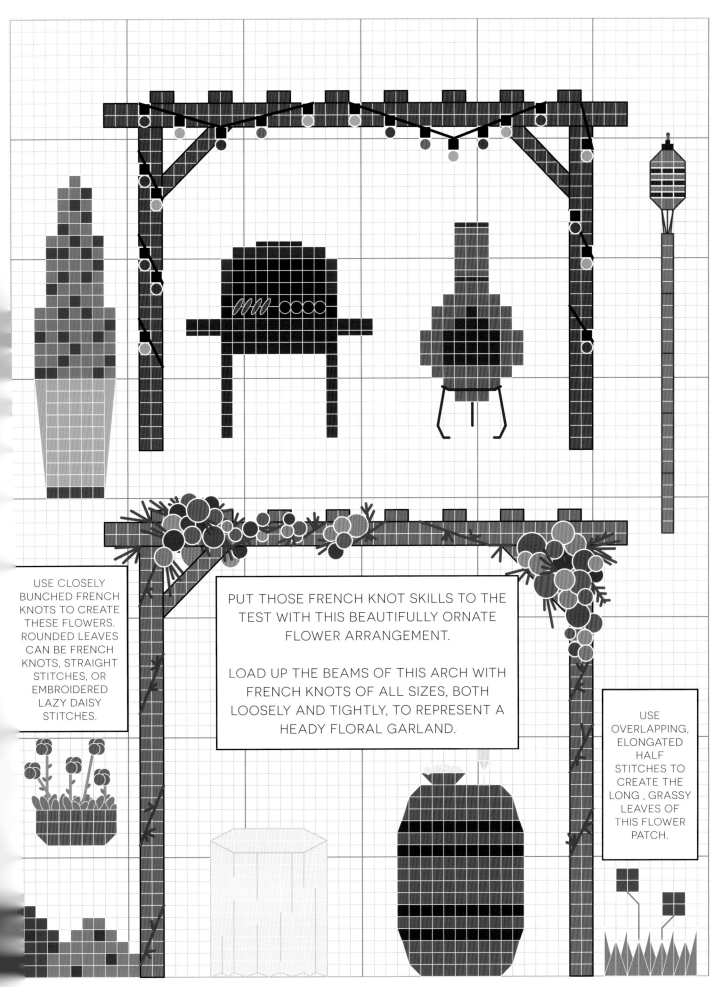

USE CLOSELY BUNCHED FRENCH KNOTS TO CREATE THESE FLOWERS. ROUNDED LEAVES CAN BE FRENCH KNOTS, STRAIGHT STITCHES, OR EMBROIDERED LAZY DAISY STITCHES.

PUT THOSE FRENCH KNOT SKILLS TO THE TEST WITH THIS BEAUTIFULLY ORNATE FLOWER ARRANGEMENT.

LOAD UP THE BEAMS OF THIS ARCH WITH FRENCH KNOTS OF ALL SIZES, BOTH LOOSELY AND TIGHTLY, TO REPRESENT A HEADY FLORAL GARLAND.

USE OVERLAPPING, ELONGATED HALF STITCHES TO CREATE THE LONG , GRASSY LEAVES OF THIS FLOWER PATCH.

# ROAD TRIPPING

The pattern below was modeled after the image to the left. The scenery utilizes patterns found in this book, in the "Open Sky" section and the "Road Tripping" section. The characters were created using patterns from "Do-It-Yourself Stitch People."

Just because you don't have all of the elements of a scene or background visible in an image doesn't mean you can't fill in the blanks, yourself!

For example, the scenery in the pattern below may not replicate exactly what those two gals saw from their windshield in the image, and the car may also not match precisely. However, setting the scene in this way allows for a fuller picture of the memory to come to life in the mind of the viewer.

After all, there's nothing wrong with a bit of "artistic interpretation" of real-life events!

TRUE TO SCALE OF SIZE 11 AIDA FABRIC: 11 SQUARES PER INCH

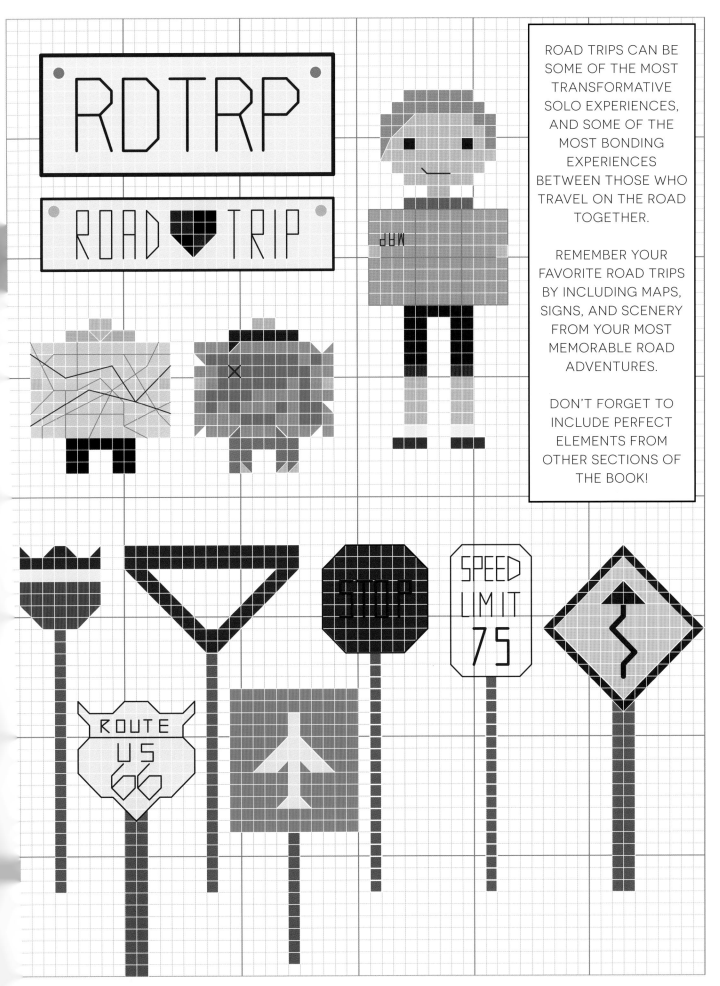

ROAD TRIPS CAN BE SOME OF THE MOST TRANSFORMATIVE SOLO EXPERIENCES, AND SOME OF THE MOST BONDING EXPERIENCES BETWEEN THOSE WHO TRAVEL ON THE ROAD TOGETHER.

REMEMBER YOUR FAVORITE ROAD TRIPS BY INCLUDING MAPS, SIGNS, AND SCENERY FROM YOUR MOST MEMORABLE ROAD ADVENTURES.

DON'T FORGET TO INCLUDE PERFECT ELEMENTS FROM OTHER SECTIONS OF THE BOOK!

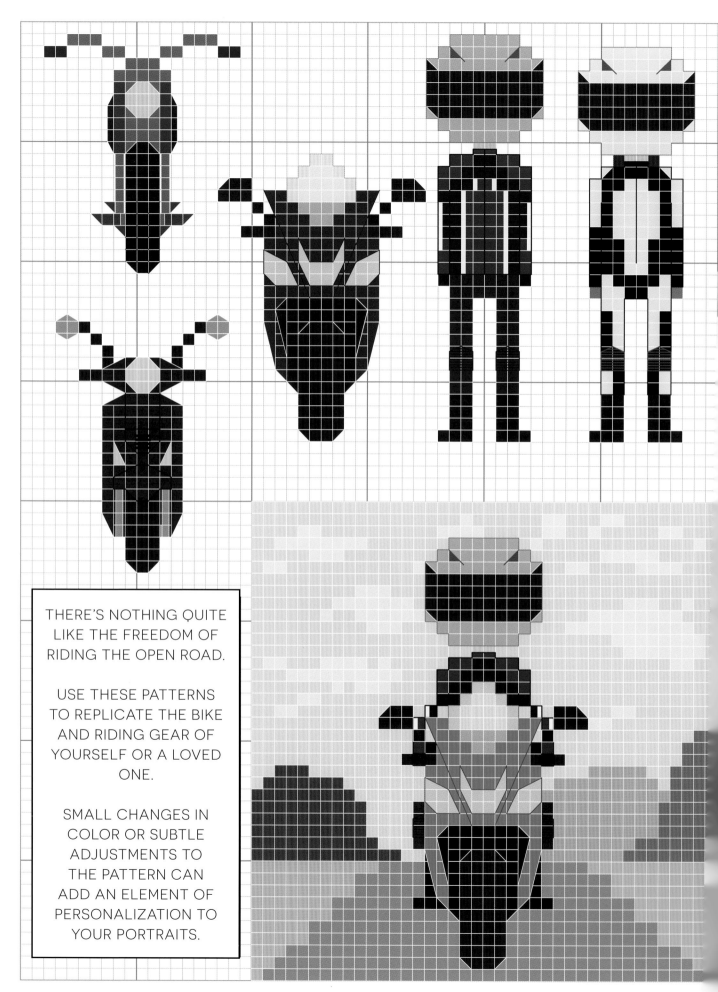

THERE'S NOTHING QUITE
LIKE THE FREEDOM OF
RIDING THE OPEN ROAD.

USE THESE PATTERNS
TO REPLICATE THE BIKE
AND RIDING GEAR OF
YOURSELF OR A LOVED
ONE.

SMALL CHANGES IN
COLOR OR SUBTLE
ADJUSTMENTS TO
THE PATTERN CAN
ADD AN ELEMENT OF
PERSONALIZATION TO
YOUR PORTRAITS.

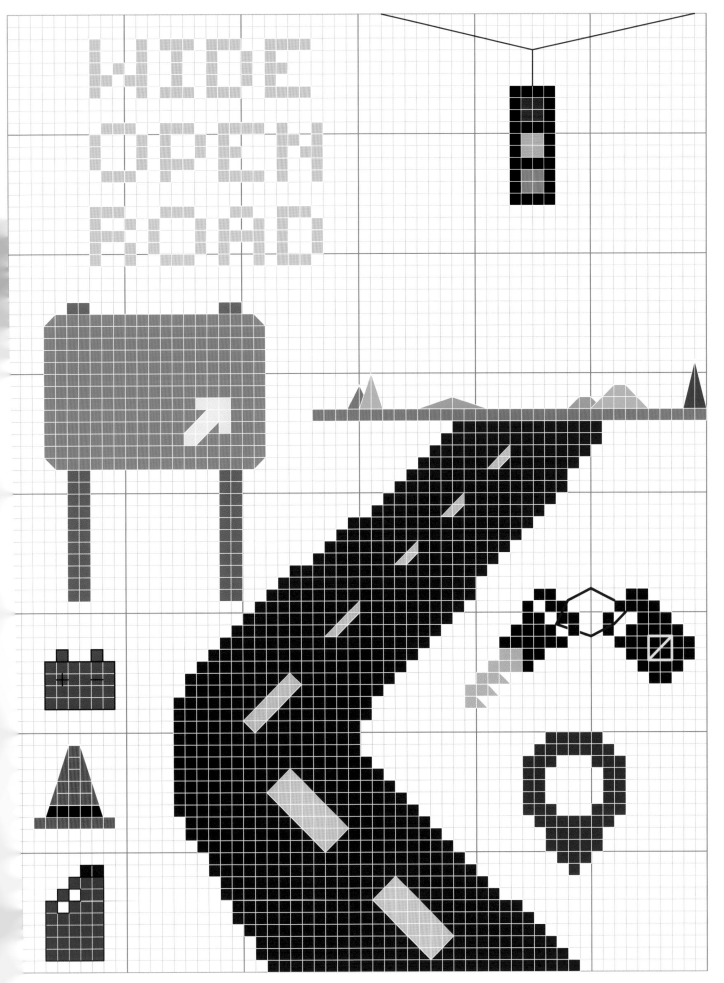

USE THIS PATTERN FOR YOUR ROAD TRIPPIN' SEDAN OR COUPE!

FOR THOSE TRIPS WHERE YOU NEED TO TAKE EXTRA BAGS, ADD A CARGO CARRIER TO THE TOP OF YOUR RIDE!

# SNOWY SCENES

The pattern below was modeled after the image to the left. The scenery utilizes patterns found in this book, in the "Camping & The Woods" section, and the "Snowy Scenes" section. The family members were created after templates found in "Do-It-Yourself-Stitch People."

Even the simplest family moments can be captured in time, and made even more memorable with a Stitch People portrait!

Do not be afraid to free-hand what you don't find in this, or other books. In the image, you can see much scraggly, twiggy regrowth at the base of the Aspen trees. These are easily created with line shapes, using 2 or 3 threads of floss. They're represented in the pattern below with diagonal lines, only, but will add even more authenticity to the portrait when it's finished.

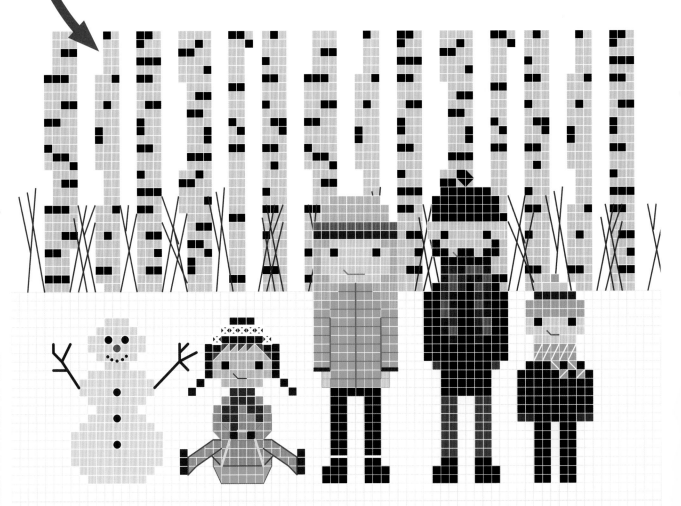

TRUE TO SCALE OF SIZE 11 AIDA FABRIC: 11 SQUARES PER INCH

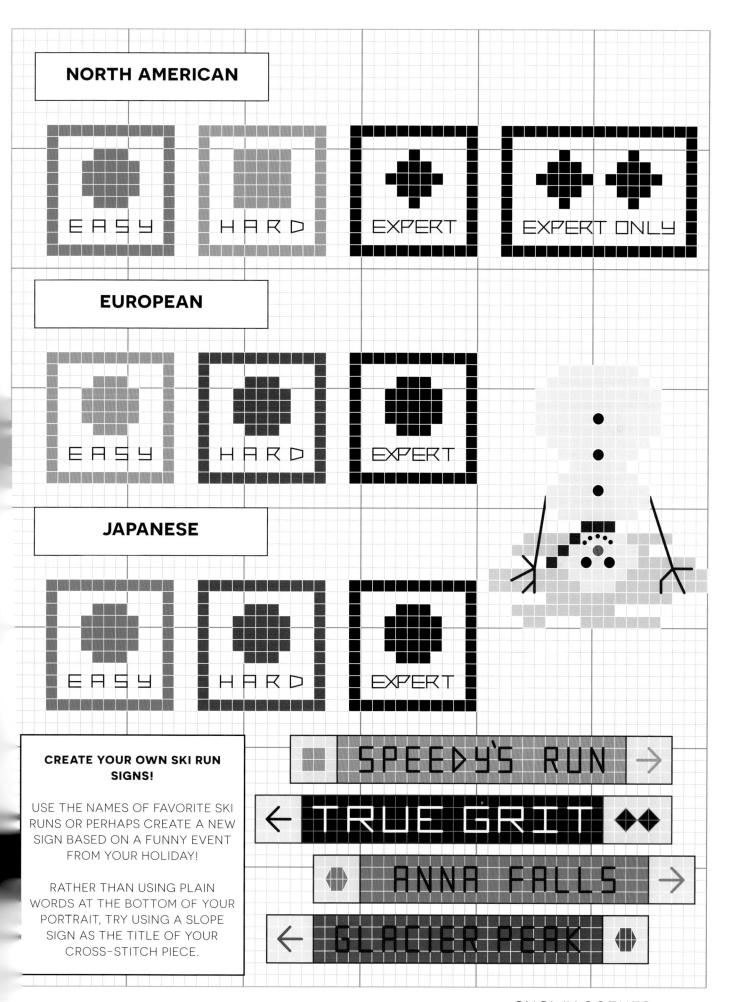

# NORTH AMERICAN

EASY  HARD  EXPERT  EXPERT ONLY

# EUROPEAN

EASY  HARD  EXPERT

# JAPANESE

EASY  HARD  EXPERT

**CREATE YOUR OWN SKI RUN SIGNS!**

USE THE NAMES OF FAVORITE SKI RUNS OR PERHAPS CREATE A NEW SIGN BASED ON A FUNNY EVENT FROM YOUR HOLIDAY!

RATHER THAN USING PLAIN WORDS AT THE BOTTOM OF YOUR PORTRAIT, TRY USING A SLOPE SIGN AS THE TITLE OF YOUR CROSS-STITCH PIECE.

SPEEDY'S RUN →

← TRUE GRIT ◆◆

ANNA FALLS →

← GLACIER PEAK

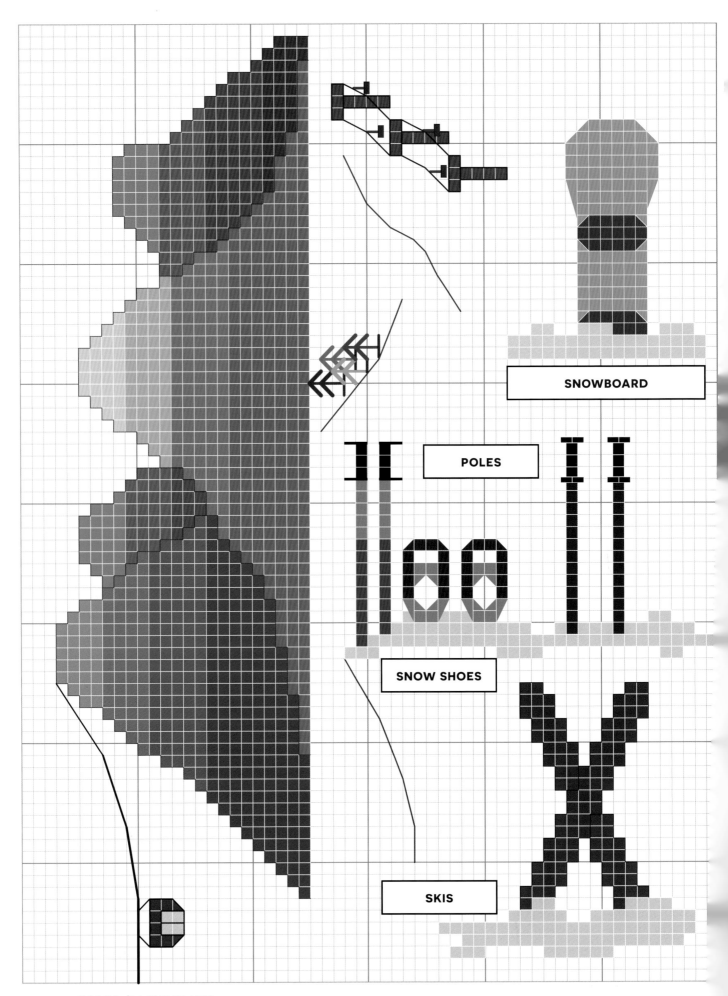

SNOWBOARD

POLES

SNOW SHOES

SKIS

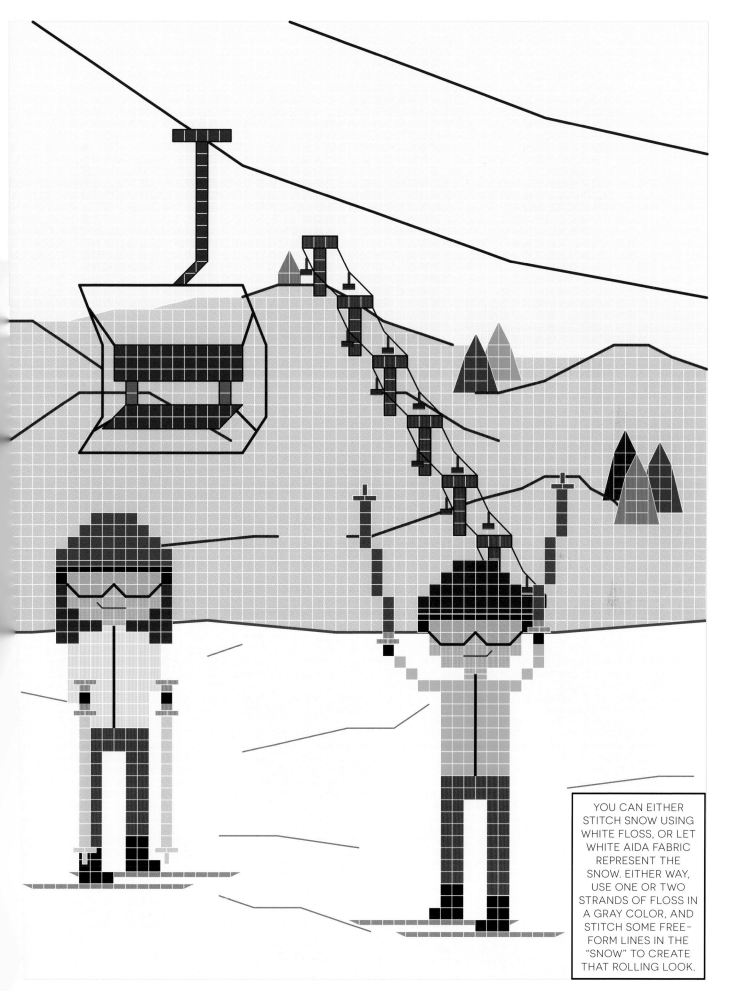

YOU CAN EITHER
STITCH SNOW USING
WHITE FLOSS, OR LET
WHITE AIDA FABRIC
REPRESENT THE
SNOW. EITHER WAY,
USE ONE OR TWO
STRANDS OF FLOSS IN
A GRAY COLOR, AND
STITCH SOME FREE-
FORM LINES IN THE
"SNOW" TO CREATE
THAT ROLLING LOOK.

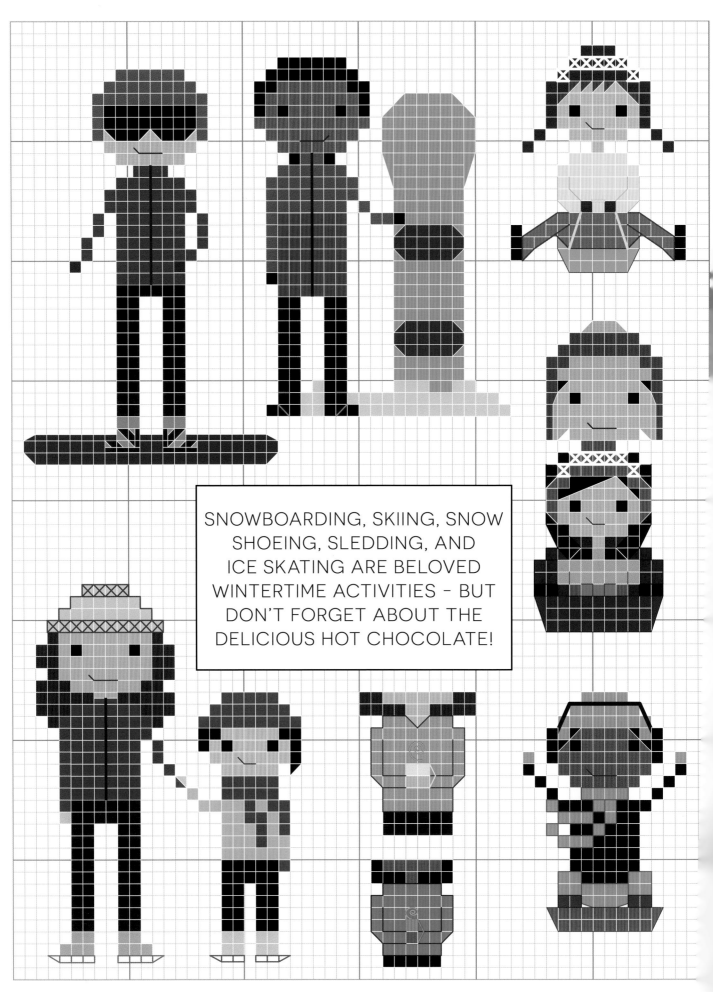

SNOWBOARDING, SKIING, SNOW SHOEING, SLEDDING, AND ICE SKATING ARE BELOVED WINTERTIME ACTIVITIES - BUT DON'T FORGET ABOUT THE DELICIOUS HOT CHOCOLATE!

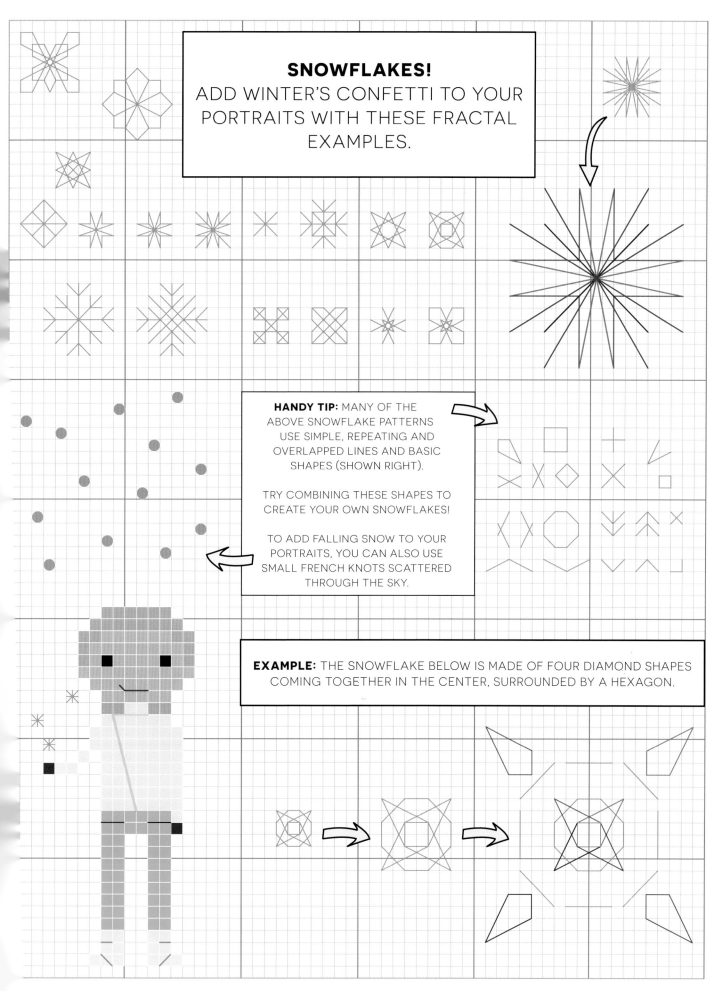

**SNOWFLAKES!**
ADD WINTER'S CONFETTI TO YOUR PORTRAITS WITH THESE FRACTAL EXAMPLES.

**HANDY TIP:** MANY OF THE ABOVE SNOWFLAKE PATTERNS USE SIMPLE, REPEATING AND OVERLAPPED LINES AND BASIC SHAPES (SHOWN RIGHT).

TRY COMBINING THESE SHAPES TO CREATE YOUR OWN SNOWFLAKES!

TO ADD FALLING SNOW TO YOUR PORTRAITS, YOU CAN ALSO USE SMALL FRENCH KNOTS SCATTERED THROUGH THE SKY.

**EXAMPLE:** THE SNOWFLAKE BELOW IS MADE OF FOUR DIAMOND SHAPES COMING TOGETHER IN THE CENTER, SURROUNDED BY A HEXAGON.

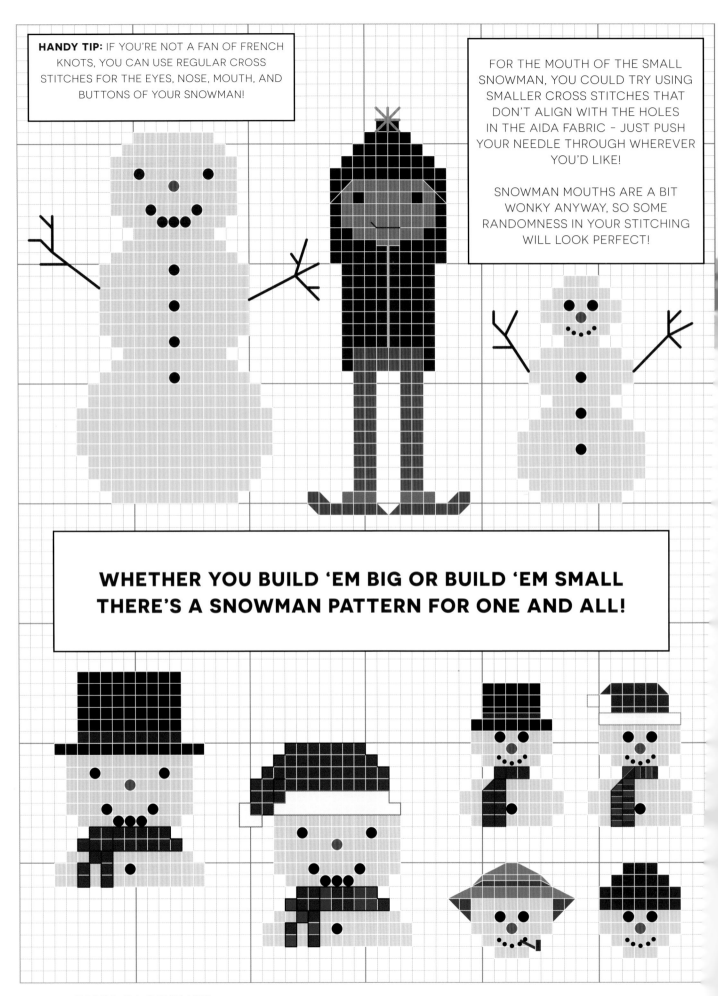

**HANDY TIP:** IF YOU'RE NOT A FAN OF FRENCH KNOTS, YOU CAN USE REGULAR CROSS STITCHES FOR THE EYES, NOSE, MOUTH, AND BUTTONS OF YOUR SNOWMAN!

FOR THE MOUTH OF THE SMALL SNOWMAN, YOU COULD TRY USING SMALLER CROSS STITCHES THAT DON'T ALIGN WITH THE HOLES IN THE AIDA FABRIC – JUST PUSH YOUR NEEDLE THROUGH WHEREVER YOU'D LIKE!

SNOWMAN MOUTHS ARE A BIT WONKY ANYWAY, SO SOME RANDOMNESS IN YOUR STITCHING WILL LOOK PERFECT!

**WHETHER YOU BUILD 'EM BIG OR BUILD 'EM SMALL THERE'S A SNOWMAN PATTERN FOR ONE AND ALL!**

# BEACHY & TROPICAL

The pattern below was modeled after the image to the left. The scenery utilizes patterns found in this book, in the "Open Sky" section, and the "Beachy & Tropical" section. The couple was created using patterns from "Do-It-Yourself-Stitch People."

Instead of customizing the patterns from this book even further to create a mirror-perfect rendition of the photo here, I used the patterns as they're found in the book to show that you can recreate a memory, photo or a scene in a non-precise way and still successfully recreate the scene, for all intents and purposes.

Is there any question that the pattern below represents the image above? No! Especially not to the couple pictured in the image. They'll instantly know the moment you're seeking to capture with your Stitch People portrait.

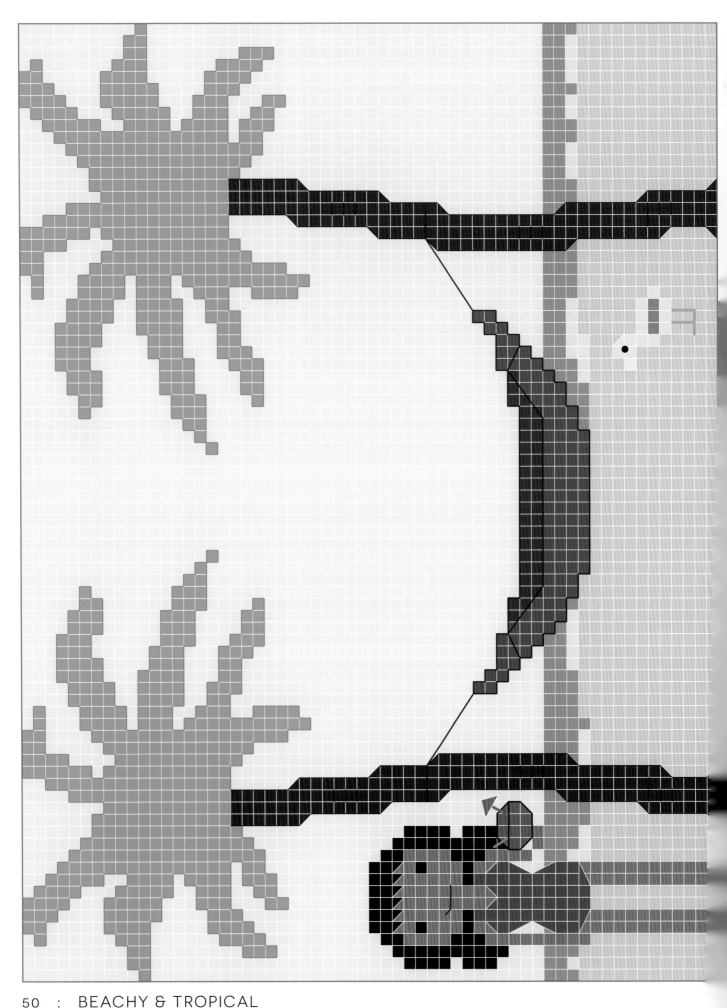

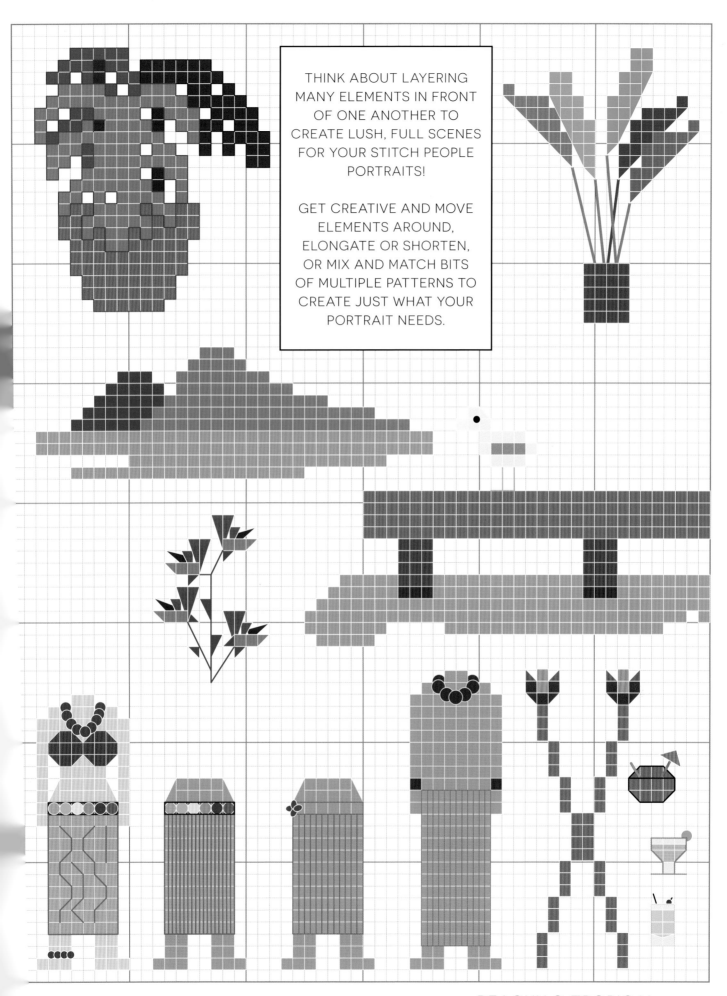

THINK ABOUT LAYERING MANY ELEMENTS IN FRONT OF ONE ANOTHER TO CREATE LUSH, FULL SCENES FOR YOUR STITCH PEOPLE PORTRAITS!

GET CREATIVE AND MOVE ELEMENTS AROUND, ELONGATE OR SHORTEN, OR MIX AND MATCH BITS OF MULTIPLE PATTERNS TO CREATE JUST WHAT YOUR PORTRAIT NEEDS.

USING A SLIGHTLY DARKER GREEN
FLOSS COLOR TO OUTLINE THE PALM
FRONDS WILL HELP THE SHAPE OF THE
LEAVES TO POP.

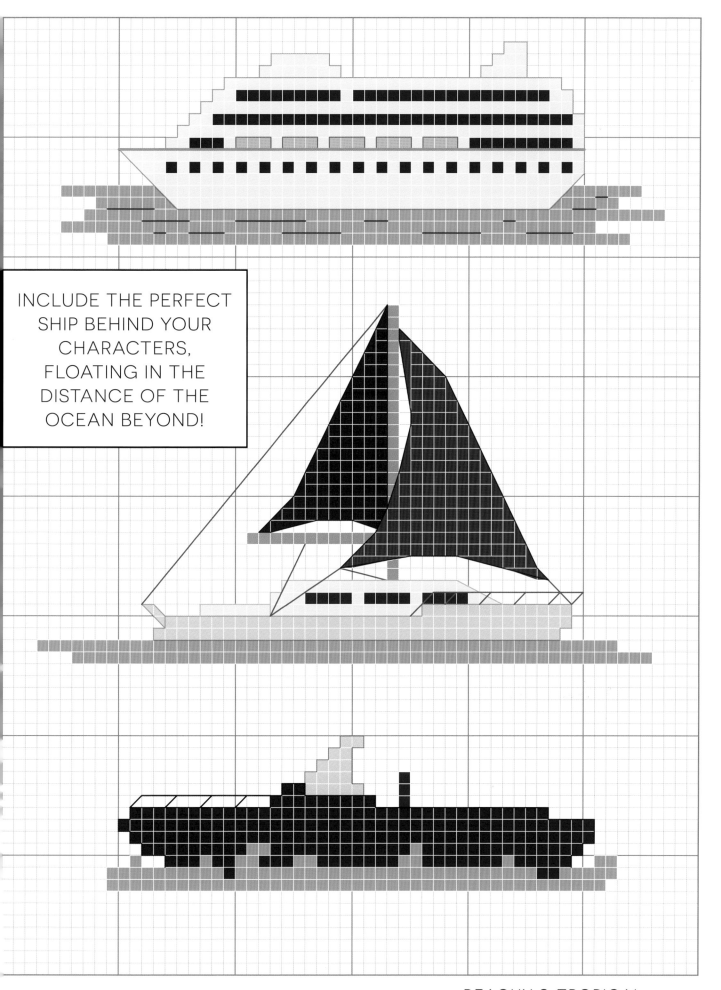

INCLUDE THE PERFECT SHIP BEHIND YOUR CHARACTERS, FLOATING IN THE DISTANCE OF THE OCEAN BEYOND!